Best-Loved
Christmas
RECIPES

D1504288

pil

Publications International, Ltd.
Favorite Brand Name Recipes at www.fbnr.com

Pictured on the front cover *(clockwise from top left):* Perfect Pumpkin Pie *(page 58)*, Country Recipe Biscuits *(page 40)*, Cherry Orange Poppy Seed Muffins *(page 38)*, Holiday Turkey with Herbed Corn Bread Dressing *(page 20)* and Oven-Roasted Peppers and Onions *(page 48)*.

Pictured on the back cover *(top to bottom):* Roasted Cornish Hen with Double Mushroom Stuffing *(page 28)*, Apricot-Cranberry Holiday Bread *(page 36)* and Hot Buttered Cider *(page 16)*.

Microwave Cooking: Microwave ovens vary in wattage. Use the cooking times as guidelines and check for doneness before adding more time.

Preparation/Cooking Times: Preparation times are based on the approximate amount of time required to assemble the recipe before cooking, baking, chilling or serving. These times include preparation steps such as measuring, chopping and mixing. The fact that some preparations and cooking can be done simultaneously is taken into account. Preparation of optional ingredients and serving suggestions is not included.

Contents

Festive Starts

Triple Delicious Hot Chocolate

⅓ cup sugar
¼ cup unsweetened cocoa powder
¼ teaspoon salt
3 cups milk, divided
¾ teaspoon vanilla extract
1 cup heavy cream
1 square (1 ounce) bittersweet chocolate
1 square (1 ounce) white chocolate
¾ cup whipped cream
6 teaspoons mini chocolate chips or
    shaved bittersweet chocolate

1. Combine sugar, cocoa, salt and ½ cup milk in medium bowl. Beat until smooth. Pour into slow cooker. Add remaining 2½ cups milk and vanilla. Cover and cook on LOW 2 hours.

2. Add cream. Cover and cook on LOW 10 minutes. Stir in bittersweet and white chocolates.

3. Pour hot chocolate into 6 coffee cups. Top each with 2 tablespoons whipped cream and 1 teaspoon chocolate chips.

Makes 6 servings

Quick Hot Spiced Cider

8 cups MOTT'S® Apple Juice
2 tablespoons brown sugar
1 teaspoon whole allspice
1 teaspoon whole cloves
8 cinnamon sticks

Combine apple juice, brown sugar, allspice and cloves in large pot. Bring to boil, then simmer 15 minutes. Remove cloves and allspice. Add cinnamon stick to each mug before serving. *Makes 8 servings*

Triple Delicious Hot Chocolate

Barbecued Swedish Meatballs

Meatballs
- 1½ pounds lean ground beef
- 1 cup finely chopped onions
- ½ cup fresh breadcrumbs
- ½ cup HOLLAND HOUSE® White Cooking Wine
- 1 egg, beaten
- ½ teaspoon allspice
- ½ teaspoon nutmeg

Sauce
- 1 jar (10 ounces) currant jelly
- ½ cup chili sauce
- ¼ cup HOLLAND HOUSE® White Cooking Wine
- 1 tablespoon cornstarch

Heat oven to 350°F. In medium bowl, combine all meatball ingredients; mix well. Shape into 1-inch balls. Place meatballs in 15×10×1-inch baking pan. Bake 20 minutes or until brown.

In medium saucepan, combine all sauce ingredients; mix well. Cook over medium heat until mixture boils and thickens, stirring occasionally. Add meatballs. To serve, place in fondue pot or chafing dish. Serve with cocktail picks. *Makes 6 to 8 servings*

Roasted Red Pepper Stuffed Mushrooms

- 1 pound medium-sized fresh white mushrooms
- 1 package (8 ounces) cream cheese, softened
- ¼ cup roasted red peppers, patted dry
- 2 tablespoons grated Parmesan cheese
- 1 teaspoon minced garlic
  Pinch ground red pepper
  Toasted pine nuts, sliced green olives and parsley leaves, for garnish (optional)

Remove stems from mushrooms; reserve caps. Set stems aside for another use. Place cream cheese, roasted red peppers, Parmesan cheese, garlic and ground red pepper in food processor fitted with metal blade; process until smooth. Place cream cheese mixture in pastry bag fitted with large star tip. Pipe into mushroom caps; garnish with pine nuts, green olives and parsley leaves, if desired.
Makes about 2 dozen mushrooms

*Favorite recipe from **Mushroom Council***

Barbecued Swedish Meatballs

Holiday Cheese Tree

1½ packages (12 ounces) cream cheese, softened
3 cups (12 ounces) shredded Cheddar cheese
5 tablespoons finely chopped red bell pepper
5 tablespoons finely chopped onion
4½ teaspoons lemon juice
3 teaspoons Worcestershire sauce
1¼ cups chopped fresh parsley
Yellow bell pepper
Cherry tomatoes, halved
Lemon peel, cut into strips

1. Combine cheeses, chopped red bell pepper, onion, lemon juice and Worcestershire in medium bowl; mix until well blended. Place on plate. Shape with hands to form cone shape, about 8 inches tall.

2. Press parsley evenly onto cheese tree.

3. Using small star-shaped cookie cutter, cut star from yellow bell pepper. Place on top of cheese tree. Decorate tree with tomato halves and lemon peel as desired.

Makes about 7½ cups
(20 to 24 appetizer servings)

Classic Chicken Puffs

1 box UNCLE BEN'S® Long Grain & Wild
   Rice Original Recipe
2 cups cubed cooked TYSON® Fresh
   Chicken
½ can (10¾ ounces) condensed cream of
   mushroom soup
⅓ cup chopped green onions
⅓ cup diced pimientos or diced red bell
   pepper
⅓ cup diced celery
⅓ cup chopped fresh parsley
⅓ cup chopped slivered almonds
¼ cup milk
1 box frozen prepared puff pastry shells,
   thawed

COOK: CLEAN: Wash hands. Prepare rice
according to package directions. When rice is
done, add remaining ingredients (except pastry
shells). Mix well. Reheat 1 minute. Fill pastry
shells with rice mixture.

SERVE: Serve with a mixed green salad and
balsamic vinaigrette, if desired.

CHILL: Refrigerate leftovers immediately.
Makes 6 servings

Festive Bacon & Cheese Dip

2 packages (8 ounces each) cream cheese,
   softened and cut into cubes
4 cups shredded Colby-Jack cheese
1 cup half-and-half
2 tablespoons mustard
1 tablespoon chopped onion
2 teaspoons Worcestershire sauce
½ teaspoon salt
¼ teaspoon hot pepper sauce
1 pound bacon, cooked and crumbled

Slow Cooker Directions
Place cream cheese, Colby-Jack cheese, half-
and-half, mustard, onion, Worcestershire, salt
and pepper sauce in slow cooker. Cover and
cook, stirring occasionally, on LOW 1 hour or
until cheese melts. Stir in bacon; adjust
seasonings. Serve with crusty bread or fruit
and vegetable dippers.

Makes about 1 quart

Classic Chicken Puffs

Little Christmas Pizzas

⅓ **cup olive oil**
1 **tablespoon TABASCO® brand Pepper Sauce**
2 **large cloves garlic, minced**
1 **teaspoon dried rosemary, crushed**
1 **(16-ounce) package hot roll mix with yeast packet**
1¼ **cups hot water***
Flour

Toppings
1 **large tomato, diced**
¼ **cup crumbled goat cheese**
2 **tablespoons chopped fresh parsley**
½ **cup shredded mozzarella cheese**
½ **cup pitted green olives**
⅓ **cup roasted red pepper strips**
½ **cup chopped artichoke hearts**
½ **cup cherry tomatoes, sliced into wedges**
⅓ **cup sliced green onions**

*Check hot roll mix package directions for temperature of water.

Combine olive oil, TABASCO® Sauce, garlic and rosemary in small bowl. Combine hot roll mix, yeast packet, hot water and 2 tablespoons TABASCO® Sauce mixture in large bowl; stir until dough pulls away from side of bowl. Turn dough onto lightly floured surface; shape dough into a ball. Knead until smooth, adding additional flour as necessary.

Preheat oven to 425°F. Cut dough into quarters; cut each quarter into 10 equal pieces. Roll each piece into a ball. On large cookie sheet, press each ball into 2-inch round. Brush each with remaining TABASCO® Sauce mixture. Arrange approximately 2 teaspoons toppings on each dough round. Bake 12 minutes or until dough is lightly browned and puffed.

Makes 40 appetizer servings

Deviled Eggs

6 **hard-cooked eggs, cut lengthwise**
¼ **cup mayonnaise**
¼ **to ½ teaspoon LAWRY'S® Seasoned Salt**
⅛ **teaspoon white pepper**
Paprika (garnish)

Remove yolks from eggs; place yolks in small bowl. Mash or crumble with fork; add remaining ingredients. Whip with fork until smooth. Place in pastry bag; pipe mixture into egg white centers. *Makes 12 eggs*

Serving Suggestion: Garnish with paprika and serve on a lettuce-lined platter.

Festive Egg Nog

6 cups skim milk, divided
1 cup EGG BEATERS® Healthy Real Egg
    Product
½ cup sugar
1 teaspoon vanilla extract
1 teaspoon rum extract
¼ cup brandy, optional
    Ground nutmeg and cinnamon, for
    garnish

In large saucepan, over medium heat, heat 5 cups milk, Egg Beaters® and sugar until thickened, stirring constantly. Remove from heat; stir in vanilla and rum extracts. Cover; chill at least 3 hours.

Just before serving, stir in brandy if desired; thin to desired consistency with remaining milk. Garnish with sprinkle of nutmeg and cinnamon.   *Makes 8 servings*

Prep Time: 15 minutes
Cook Time: 25 minutes

Sparkling White Sangria

1 cup KARO® Light Corn Syrup
1 orange, sliced
1 lemon, sliced
1 lime, sliced
½ cup orange-flavored liqueur
1 bottle (750 ml) dry white wine
2 tablespoons lemon juice
1 bottle (12 ounces) club soda or seltzer,
    chilled
Additional fresh fruit (optional)

1. In large pitcher combine corn syrup, orange, lemon and lime slices and liqueur. Let stand 20 to 30 minutes, stirring occasionally.

2. Stir in wine and lemon juice. Refrigerate.

3. Just before serving, add soda and ice cubes. If desired, garnish with additional fruit.
          Makes about 6 (8-ounce) servings

Prep Time: 15 minutes, plus standing and chilling

Easiest Three-Cheese Fondue

  1 tablespoon margarine
¼ cup finely chopped onion
  2 cloves garlic, minced
  1 tablespoon all-purpose flour
¾ cup reduced-fat (2%) milk
  2 cups (8 ounces) shredded mild or sharp
      Cheddar cheese
  1 package (3 ounces) cream cheese, cut
      into cubes
½ cup (2 ounces) crumbled blue cheese
⅛ teaspoon ground red pepper
  4 to 6 drops hot pepper sauce
      Breadsticks and assorted fresh vegetables
      for dipping

1. Heat margarine in small saucepan over medium heat until melted. Add onion and garlic; cook and stir 2 to 3 minutes or until tender. Stir in flour; cook 2 minutes, stirring constantly.

2. Stir milk into saucepan; bring to a boil. Boil, stirring constantly, about 1 minute or until thickened. Reduce heat to low; add cheeses, stirring until melted. Stir in red pepper and pepper sauce. Pour fondue into serving dish. Serve with dippers.

Makes 8 (3-tablespoon) servings

Hot Buttered Cider

⅓ cup packed brown sugar
¼ cup butter or margarine, softened
¼ cup honey
¼ teaspoon ground cinnamon
¼ teaspoon ground nutmeg
     Apple cider or juice

1. Beat sugar, butter, honey, cinnamon and nutmeg until well blended and fluffy. Place butter mixture in tightly covered container. Refrigerate up to 2 weeks. Bring butter mixture to room temperature before using.

2. To serve, heat apple cider in large saucepan over medium heat until hot. Fill individual mugs with hot apple cider; stir in 1 tablespoon butter mixture per 1 cup apple cider. Garnish as desired. *Makes 12 servings*

Prep and Cook Time: 15 minutes

Hot Buttered Cider

Mini Crab Cakes

 1 pound crabmeat
 1 cup fine, dry bread crumbs, divided
 2 eggs, beaten
 ¼ cup minced onion
 ¼ cup minced green bell pepper
 ¼ cup minced red bell pepper
 1 teaspoon dry mustard
 ½ teaspoon TABASCO® brand Pepper Sauce
   Salt to taste
   Vegetable oil
   Zesty Remoulade Sauce (recipe follows)
   Fresh dill (optional)

Combine crabmeat, ½ cup bread crumbs, eggs, onion, bell peppers, mustard, TABASCO® Sauce and salt in large bowl. Cover and refrigerate 1 to 2 hours or until mixture becomes firm. Shape mixture into small cakes, about 1×1½ inches. Coat cakes in remaining ½ cup bread crumbs.

Pour oil into heavy skillet to depth of ⅓ inch; heat skillet over medium heat. When oil is hot, cook crab cakes about 3 to 5 minutes on each side or until browned. Remove to paper towels. Serve crab cakes warm; top with dollops of Zesty Remoulade Sauce. Garnish with dill sprigs, if desired.

Makes 20 to 25 cakes

Zesty Remoulade Sauce

 1 cup mayonnaise
 2 to 3 green onions, finely chopped
 1 celery stalk, finely chopped
 2 tablespoons prepared horseradish, drained
 1 tablespoon finely chopped chives
 1 tablespoon Dijon mustard
 1 tablespoon fresh lemon juice
 1 clove garlic, finely chopped
 ½ teaspoon TABASCO® brand Pepper Sauce

Combine all ingredients in medium bowl. Cover and refrigerate 1 hour to blend flavors. Serve chilled. *Makes 1¾ cups*

Holiday Wassail

 1 gallon MOTT'S® Apple Juice
 1 quart orange juice
 1 can (16 ounces) frozen pineapple juice, thawed
 2 cups lemon juice
 1 cup sugar
 2 cinnamon sticks
 2 teaspoons cloves

Place all ingredients in non-aluminum pan, stir, and heat to boiling. Simmer for one hour. Serve hot. *Makes 24 servings*

Mini Crab Cakes

Merry Main Dishes

Holiday Turkey with Herbed Corn Bread Dressing

    1 pound bulk pork sausage
1½ cups chopped onions
    1 cup chopped celery
    6 cups coarsely crumbled corn bread (two
        8-inch squares)
⅓ cup light cream
¼ cup sherry
    1 teaspoon dried thyme leaves
    1 teaspoon dried basil leaves
    1 teaspoon dried oregano leaves
½ teaspoon LAWRY'S® Garlic Powder with
        Parsley
    1 (14- to 16-pound) turkey, thawed
        LAWRY'S® Seasoned Salt

In large skillet, cook sausage until brown and crumbly. Add onions and celery and cook over medium heat 5 minutes or until tender. Add corn bread, cream, sherry, thyme, basil, oregano and Garlic Powder with Parsley. Rub cavity and outside of turkey with Seasoned Salt, using about ¼ teaspoon Seasoned Salt per pound of turkey. Pack dressing loosely into turkey cavity. Skewer opening closed. Insert meat thermometer in thickest part of breast away from bones. Place turkey, breast side up, on rack in roasting pan. Roast, uncovered, in 325°F oven 4 to 5 hours, basting frequently with melted butter, or cover with foil and place on hot grill 16 to 18 minutes per pound. When internal temperature reaches 185°F, remove and let stand 20 minutes before carving. (Tent loosely with aluminum foil if turkey becomes too brown, being careful not to touch meat thermometer.)   *Makes 10 servings*

Serving Suggestion: Garnish with lemon leaves and whole fresh cranberries.

Holiday Turkey with Herbed Corn Bread Dressing

Prime Rib with Yorkshire Pudding and Horseradish Cream Sauce

- **3 cloves garlic, minced**
- **1 teaspoon black pepper**
- **3 rib standing beef roast, trimmed* (about 6 to 7 pounds)**
- **Yorkshire Pudding (recipe follows)**
- **Horseradish Cream Sauce (page 24)**

*Ask meat retailer to remove the chine bone for easier carving. Fat should be trimmed to ¼-inch thickness.

Preheat oven to 450°F. Combine garlic and pepper; rub over surfaces of roast.

Place roast, bone side down (the bones take the place of a meat rack), in shallow roasting pan. Roast 15 minutes.

Reduce oven temperature to 325°F. Roast 20 minutes per pound for medium or until internal temperature reaches 145°F when tested with meat thermometer inserted into thickest part of roast, not touching bone.

Meanwhile, prepare Yorkshire Pudding and Horseradish Cream Sauce.

When roast has reached desired temperature, transfer to cutting board; cover with foil. Let stand 10 to 15 minutes before carving. Internal temperature will continue to rise 5°F to 10°F during stand time.

Reserve ¼ cup drippings from roasting pan for Yorkshire Pudding. Immediately after roast has been removed from oven, *increase oven temperature to 450°F.*

While pudding is baking, carve roast. Serve with Yorkshire Pudding and Horseradish Cream Sauce. *Makes 6 to 8 servings*

Yorkshire Pudding

- **1 cup milk**
- **2 eggs**
- **½ teaspoon salt**
- **1 cup all-purpose flour**
- **¼ cup reserved drippings from roast or unsalted butter**

Process milk, eggs and salt in blender or food processor 15 seconds. Add flour; process 2 minutes. Let batter stand in blender at room temperature 30 minutes to 1 hour.

continued on page 24

Prime Rib with Yorkshire Pudding and Horseradish Cream Sauce

Prime Rib with Yorkshire Pudding and Horseradish Cream Sauce, *continued from page 22*

Place reserved meat drippings in 9-inch square baking pan. Place in 450°F oven 5 minutes.

Process batter another 10 seconds; pour into hot drippings. Do not stir.

Immediately return pan to oven. Bake 20 minutes. *Reduce oven temperature to 350°F;* bake 10 minutes or until pudding is golden brown and puffed. Cut into squares.

Makes 6 to 8 servings

Horseradish Cream Sauce

1 cup whipping cream
$\frac{1}{3}$ cup prepared horseradish, undrained
2 teaspoons balsamic or red wine vinegar
1 teaspoon dry mustard
$\frac{1}{4}$ teaspoon sugar
$\frac{1}{8}$ teaspoon salt

Beat cream until soft peaks form. *Do not overbeat.* Combine horseradish, vinegar, mustard, sugar and salt in medium bowl. Fold whipped cream into horseradish mixture. Cover and refrigerate at least 1 hour. Sauce may be made up to 8 hours before serving.

Makes 1½ cups

Festive Stuffed Fish

2 whole red snappers, about 2¼ pounds each (or substitute any firm white fish), cleaned
  Lemon and lime wedges
2 cloves garlic, minced
2 tablespoons olive oil
2 medium onions, finely chopped
1 cup seeded and chopped medium-hot pepper (such as poblano, serrano, Anaheim or green bell variety)
1 cup chopped red bell pepper
8 ounces JARLSBERG or JARLSBERG LITE™ Cheese, shredded
12 tomatillos, thinly sliced, then chopped (about 2 cups)
1 cup dry white wine or unsweetened apple juice
  Additional lemon and lime wedges

Score flesh on each fish ¼ inch deep on the diagonal every 1½ inches. Insert lemon wedges, peel side out. Cook garlic in olive oil in medium skillet over medium-high heat. Add onions and cook until translucent. Add peppers; cook 2 minutes. Place in large bowl; stir in cheese and tomatillos. Stuff fish cavity with cheese mixture. Use kitchen string to tie each fish closed every 2 inches (3 or 4 ties). Set aside. Preheat oven to 375°F.

In same skillet, bring wine to a boil. Place fish in large glass or enamel baking dish. Pour hot wine over fish and cover tightly.

Bake 30 minutes or until fish is opaque. Transfer to serving platter and remove string. Garnish with additional lemon and lime wedges. *Makes 4 to 6 servings*

Herb Crusted Racks of Lamb

>   2 American lamb racks (8 ribs each), frenched and trimmed
>   1 cup finely chopped parsley
>   1 medium onion, finely chopped
>   ¼ cup fine dry bread crumbs
>   1 tablespoon fresh dill weed, chopped, *or* 1 teaspoon dried dill weed
>   2 teaspoons fresh oregano leaves, chopped, *or* ½ teaspoon dried oregano
>   1 teaspoon salt
>   ⅛ teaspoon ground pepper

Preheat oven to 425°F. Combine all ingredients, except lamb; mix well. Pat mixture on outside of lamb.

Place on broiler rack in shallow roasting pan. Roast 40 minutes for medium-rare (145° to 150°F). *Makes 4 servings*

Favorite recipe from **American Lamb Council**

Pork Roast with Corn Bread & Oyster Stuffing

>   1 (5- to 7-pound) pork loin roast*
>   2 tablespoons butter *or* margarine
>   ½ cup chopped onion
>   ½ cup chopped celery
>   2 cloves garlic, minced
>   ½ teaspoon fennel seeds, crushed
>   1 teaspoon TABASCO® brand Pepper Sauce
>   ½ teaspoon salt
>   2 cups packaged corn bread stuffing mix
>   1 (8-ounce) can oysters, undrained, chopped

*Have butcher crack backbone of pork loin roast.

Preheat oven to 325°F. Make a deep slit in back of each chop on pork loin. Melt butter in large saucepan; add onion, celery, garlic and fennel. Cook 5 minutes or until vegetables are tender; stir in TABASCO® Sauce and salt. Add stuffing mix, oysters and oyster liquid; toss to mix well.

Stuff mixture into slits in pork. (Leftover stuffing may be baked in covered baking dish during last 30 minutes of roasting.) Place meat in shallow roasting pan. Cook 30 to 35 minutes per pound or until meat thermometer inserted into roast registers 170°F. Remove to heated serving platter. Allow to stand 15 minutes before serving. *Makes 12 servings*

Chicken Stew with Dumplings

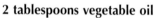

- 2 tablespoons vegetable oil
- 2 cups sliced carrots
- 1 cup chopped onion
- 1 large green bell pepper, sliced
- ½ cup sliced celery
- 2 cans (about 14 ounces each) fat-free reduced-sodium chicken broth, divided
- ¼ cup plus 2 tablespoons all-purpose flour
- 2 pounds boneless skinless chicken breasts, cut into 1-inch pieces
- 3 medium potatoes, unpeeled, cut into 1-inch pieces
- 6 ounces mushrooms, halved
- ¾ cup frozen peas
- 1 teaspoon dried basil leaves
- ¾ teaspoon dried rosemary
- ¼ teaspoon dried tarragon
- ¾ to 1 teaspoon salt
- ¼ teaspoon black pepper

Herb Dumplings

- 2 cups biscuit mix
- ½ teaspoon dried basil leaves
- ½ teaspoon dried rosemary
- ¼ teaspoon dried tarragon
- ⅔ cup reduced-fat (2%) milk

1. Heat oil in 4-quart Dutch oven over medium heat until hot. Add carrots, onion, bell pepper and celery; cook and stir 5 minutes or until onion is tender. Stir in chicken broth, reserving ½ cup; bring to a boil. Mix reserved ½ cup broth and flour in small bowl; stir into boiling mixture. Boil, stirring constantly, 1 minute or until thickened. Stir chicken, potatoes, mushrooms, peas and herbs into mixture. Reduce heat to low; simmer, covered, 18 to 20 minutes or until vegetables are almost tender and chicken is no longer pink in center. Add salt and black pepper.

2. For Herb Dumplings, combine biscuit mix and herbs in small bowl; stir in milk to form soft dough. Spoon dumpling mixture on top of stew in 8 large spoonfuls. Reduce heat to low. Cook, uncovered, 10 minutes. Cover and cook 10 minutes or until biscuits are tender and toothpick inserted into center comes out clean. Serve in shallow bowls.   *Makes 8 servings*

Make-Ahead Time: up to 2 days before serving
Final Prep and Cook Time: 30 minutes

Chicken Stew with Dumpling

Roasted Cornish Hens with Double Mushroom Stuffing

  2 Cornish hens (about 1½ pounds each)
½ teaspoon salt
¼ teaspoon ground black pepper
3 tablespoons I CAN'T BELIEVE IT'S NOT BUTTER!® Spread
1 tablespoon finely chopped shallot or onion
2 teaspoons chopped fresh tarragon leaves or ½ teaspoon dried tarragon leaves, crushed (optional)
½ lemon, cut in 2 wedges
  Double Mushroom Stuffing (recipe on page 30)
1 tablespoon all-purpose flour

Preheat oven to 425°F. Season hens and hen cavities with salt and pepper.

In small bowl, blend I Can't Believe It's Not Butter! Spread, shallot and tarragon. Evenly spread under skin, then place 1 lemon wedge in each hen.

In 18×12-inch roasting pan, on rack, arrange hens breast side up; tie legs together with string. Roast uncovered 15 minutes.

Meanwhile, prepare Double Mushroom Stuffing.

Decrease heat to 350°F and place Double Mushroom Stuffing casserole in oven with hens. Continue roasting hens 30 minutes or until meat thermometer inserted in thickest part of the thigh reaches 180°F and stuffing is golden. Remove hens to serving platter and keep warm. Remove rack from pan.

Skim fat from pan drippings. Blend flour with reserved broth from stuffing; stir into pan drippings. Place roasting pan over heat and bring to a boil over high heat, stirring frequently. Reduce heat to low and simmer, stirring occasionally, 1 minute or until gravy is thickened. Serve gravy and stuffing with hens.

Makes 2 servings

Roasted Cornish Hen with Double Mushroom Stuffing

Double Mushroom Stuffing

- **3 tablespoons I CAN'T BELIEVE IT'S NOT BUTTER!® Spread**
- **½ cup chopped onion**
- **2 cups sliced white and/or shiitake mushrooms**
- **2½ cups fresh ½-inch Italian or French bread cubes**
- **1 can (14½ ounces) chicken broth**
- **2 tablespoons chopped fresh parsley**

In 12-inch nonstick skillet, melt I Can't Believe It's Not Butter! Spread over medium-high heat and cook onion, stirring occasionally, 2 minutes or until softened. Add mushrooms and cook, stirring occasionally, 4 minutes or until golden. Stir in bread, ¾ cup broth (reserve remaining broth) and parsley. Season, if desired, with salt and ground black pepper. Spoon into greased 1-quart casserole.

During last 30 minutes of roasting, place stuffing casserole in oven with hens. Cook until stuffing is heated through and golden.

Makes 2 servings

Beef Wellington

- **6 center cut beef tenderloin steaks, cut 1 inch thick (about 2½ pounds)**
- **¾ teaspoon salt, divided**
- **½ teaspoon black pepper, divided**
- **2 tablespoons butter or margarine**
- **8 ounces crimini or button mushrooms, finely chopped**
- **¼ cup finely chopped shallots or sweet onion**
- **2 tablespoons ruby port or sweet Madeira wine**
- **1 package (17¼ ounces) frozen puff pastry, thawed**
- **1 egg, separated**
- **½ cup (4 ounces) purchased liver pâté, liver pâté with cognac or chicken liver mousse***
- **2 teaspoons water**
- **Baby pattypan squash (optional)**
- **Fresh currant and pineapple sage leaves for garnish (optional)**

*Pâté can be found in the gourmet or deli section of most supermarkets or in specialty food stores.

1. Sprinkle steaks with ½ teaspoon salt and ¼ teaspoon pepper. Heat large nonstick skillet over medium-high heat until hot. Cook steaks

continued on page 32

Beef Wellington

Beef Wellington, *continued from page 30*

in batches, about 3 minutes per side or until well browned and instant-read thermometer inserted into steaks registers 110°F (very rare). Transfer to clean plate; set aside. (If meat is tied, remove string; discard.)

2. Melt butter in same skillet over medium heat; add mushrooms and shallots. Cook and stir 5 minutes or until mushrooms are tender. Add port, remaining ¼ teaspoon salt and ¼ teaspoon pepper. Bring to a boil. Reduce heat; simmer 10 minutes or until liquid evaporates, stirring often. Remove from heat; cool completely.

3. Roll out each pastry sheet to 18×10-inch rectangle on lightly floured surface with lightly floured rolling pin. Cut each sheet into 3 (10×6-inch) rectangles. Cut small amount of pastry from corners to use as decoration, if desired.

4. Beat egg white in small bowl with whisk until foamy; brush over each pastry rectangle with pastry brush. Place 1 cooled steak on each pastry rectangle. Spread pâté over steaks, dividing evenly; top with mushroom mixture, pressing lightly so mushrooms adhere to pâté.

5. Carefully turn each steak over, mushroom side down. Fold pastry over steak. Fold edge of bottom dough over top; press edges to seal. Place on ungreased baking sheet. Repeat with remaining steaks and pastries.

6. Beat egg yolk and water in small bowl; brush evenly over pastry. Cut pastry scraps into decorative shapes and decorate pastry covering steaks, if desired. Brush decorations with egg yolk mixture. Cover loosely with plastic wrap; refrigerate 1 to 4 hours or until cold.

7. Preheat oven to 400°F. Bake 20 to 25 minutes or until pastry is puffed and golden brown and steaks are medium, or when internal temperature reaches 145°F when tested with a meat thermometer. Let stand 10 minutes before serving. Serve with squash, if desired. Garnish, if desired.

Makes 6 servings

Cranberry-Orange Chicken

1 envelope SHAKE 'N BAKE® Seasoning
    and Coating Mixture—Original Recipe
    for Chicken
1 tablespoon grated orange peel
6 boneless skinless chicken breast halves
1 cup whole berry cranberry sauce
2 tablespoons orange juice

HEAT oven to 400°F.

MIX coating mixture and orange peel in shaker bag. Coat chicken as directed on package.

BAKE 15 minutes on ungreased or foil-lined 15×10-inch metal baking pan. Mix cranberry sauce and orange juice in small bowl until well blended. Spoon over chicken. Bake 5 minutes or until chicken is cooked through.

Makes 6 servings

Prep Time: 5 minutes
Cook Time: 20 minutes

Holiday Baked Ham

1 bone-in smoked ham (8½ pounds)
1 can (20 ounces) DOLE® Pineapple Slices
1 cup apricot preserves
1 teaspoon dry mustard
½ teaspoon ground allspice
    Whole cloves
    Maraschino cherries

• Preheat oven to 325°F. Remove rind from ham. Place ham on rack in open roasting pan, fat side up. Insert meat thermometer with bulb in thickest part away from fat or bone. Roast ham in oven about 3 hours.

• Drain pineapple; reserve syrup. In small saucepan, combine syrup, preserves, mustard and allspice. Bring to a boil; continue boiling, stirring occasionally, 10 minutes. Remove ham from oven, but keep oven hot. Stud ham with cloves; brush with glaze. Using wooden picks, secure pineapple and cherries to ham. Brush again with glaze. Return ham to oven. Roast 30 minutes longer or until thermometer registers 160°F (about 25 minutes per pound total cooking time). Brush with glaze 15 minutes before done. Let ham stand 20 minutes before slicing.

Makes 8 to 10 servings

Yuletide Sides

Country Corn Bread Dressing

WESSON® No-Stick Cooking Spray
1 (12-ounce) package seasoned corn bread
  stuffing
2½ cups dry bread crumbs
2 cups chopped celery
1 cup finely chopped onion
¼ cup (½ stick) butter
½ teaspoon poultry seasoning
¼ teaspoon pepper
2 (14½-ounce) cans chicken broth
¼ cup WESSON® Vegetable Oil

Preheat oven to 375°F. Spray a 13×9×2-inch baking dish with Wesson® Cooking Spray; set aside. Combine stuffing mix and bread crumbs in a large bowl; set aside. In a medium saucepan, sauté celery and onion in butter until crisp-tender; blend in poultry seasoning and pepper. Add broth and Wesson® Oil; bring to boil for 1 minute. Add to corn bread mixture; toss lightly to coat. Spoon corn bread mixture into baking dish; bake, uncovered, for 35 to 45 minutes or until golden brown.

Makes 10 to 12 servings

Sweet-Spiced Sweet Potatoes

2 pounds sweet potatoes, peeled and cut
  into ½-inch pieces
¼ cup dark brown sugar, packed
1 teaspoon ground cinnamon
½ teaspoon ground nutmeg
⅛ teaspoon salt
2 tablespoons butter, cut into ⅛-inch
  pieces
1 teaspoon vanilla extract

Combine all ingredients except butter and vanilla in slow cooker; mix well. Cover and cook on LOW 7 hours or cook on HIGH 4 hours. Add butter and vanilla; stir to blend.

Makes 4 servings

Sweet-Spiced Sweet Potatoes

Apricot-Cranberry Holiday Bread

- ⅔ **cup milk**
- 6 **tablespoons butter or margarine, softened**
- 2½ **to 3 cups all-purpose flour, divided**
- ¼ **cup sugar**
- 1 **package active dry yeast**
- ¾ **teaspoon salt**
- ½ **teaspoon ground ginger**
- ½ **teaspoon ground nutmeg**
- 2 **eggs, divided**
- ½ **cup dried apricots, chopped**
- ½ **cup dried cranberries, chopped**
- 3 **tablespoons orange juice**
- ½ **cup pecans, toasted and coarsely chopped**
- 1 **teaspoon water**

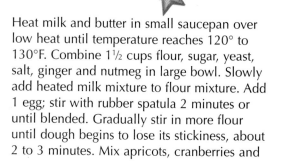

Heat milk and butter in small saucepan over low heat until temperature reaches 120° to 130°F. Combine 1½ cups flour, sugar, yeast, salt, ginger and nutmeg in large bowl. Slowly add heated milk mixture to flour mixture. Add 1 egg; stir with rubber spatula 2 minutes or until blended. Gradually stir in more flour until dough begins to lose its stickiness, about 2 to 3 minutes. Mix apricots, cranberries and orange juice in small microwavable bowl; cover with plastic wrap. Microwave at HIGH 25 to 35 seconds to soften; set aside.

Turn out dough onto floured surface. Knead 5 to 8 minutes or until smooth and elastic; gradually add remaining flour to prevent sticking, if necessary. Drain or blot apricot mixture. Combine apricot mixture and pecans in medium bowl. Flatten dough into ¾-inch-thick rectangle; sprinkle with ⅓ of fruit mixture. Roll up jelly-roll style from short end. Flatten dough; repeat twice using remaining fruit mixture. Continue to knead until blended. Shape dough into ball; place in large greased bowl. Turn dough over. Cover; let rise 1 hour or until doubled in size.

Grease 9-inch round cake or pie pan. Punch down dough; pat into 8-inch circle. Place in pan. Loosely cover with lightly greased sheet of plastic wrap. Let rise 1 hour or until doubled in size.

Preheat oven to 375°F. Beat remaining egg with 1 teaspoon water in small bowl; brush evenly over dough. Bake 30 to 35 minutes or until loaf sounds hollow when tapped. Remove immediately from pan. Cool completely on wire rack.

Makes 12 servings

Apricot-Cranberry Holiday Bread

Cherry Orange Poppy Seed Muffins

  2 cups all-purpose flour
  ³/₄ cup granulated sugar
  1 tablespoon baking powder
  1 tablespoon poppy seeds
  ¼ teaspoon salt
  1 cup milk
  ¼ cup (½ stick) butter, melted
  1 egg, slightly beaten
  ½ cup dried tart cherries
  3 tablespoons grated orange peel

Combine flour, sugar, baking powder, poppy seeds and salt in large mixing bowl. Add milk, melted butter and egg, stirring just until dry ingredients are moistened. Gently stir in cherries and orange peel. Fill paper-lined muffin cups three-fourths full.

Bake in preheated 400°F oven 18 to 22 minutes or until wooden pick inserted in center comes out clean. Let cool in pan 5 minutes. Remove from pan and serve warm or let cool completely.   *Makes 12 muffins*

Favorite recipe from **Cherry Marketing Institute**

Green Bean Casserole

  1 envelope LIPTON® RECIPE SECRETS®
     Onion Mushroom Soup Mix
  1 tablespoon all-purpose flour
  1 cup milk
  2 packages (10 ounces each) frozen cut
     green beans, thawed
  1 cup shredded Cheddar cheese (about
     4 ounces), divided
  ¼ cup plain dry bread crumbs

1. Preheat oven to 350°F. In 1½-quart casserole, combine soup mix, flour and milk; stir in green beans and ½ cup cheese.

2. Bake uncovered 25 minutes.

3. Sprinkle with bread crumbs and remaining ½ cup cheese. Bake an additional 5 minutes or until cheese is melted.

Makes 8 servings

Prep Time: 5 minutes
Cook Time: 30 minutes

Green Bean Casserole

Southwest Hopping John

1½ **cups dried black-eyed peas**
2 **tablespoons olive oil**
1 **medium onion, chopped**
4 **cloves garlic, minced**
2 **medium red or green bell peppers,
    chopped**
1 **jalapeño pepper,* minced**
1 **teaspoon ground cumin**
2½ **cups canned chicken broth**
1 **cup uncooked brown basmati rice**
¼ **pound smoked ham, diced**
4 **medium tomatoes, seeded and chopped**
½ **cup minced fresh cilantro**

*Jalapeño peppers can sting and irritate the skin; wear
rubber gloves when handling peppers and do not touch
eyes. Wash hands after handling.*

1. Rinse peas thoroughly in colander under
cold running water. Place in large bowl; cover
with 4 inches of water. Let stand at least
8 hours, then rinse and drain.

2. Transfer peas to medium saucepan; cover
with water. Bring to a boil over high heat.
Reduce heat to low; simmer, covered, 1 hour
or until tender. Drain in colander; set aside.

3. Heat oil in Dutch oven over medium-high
heat. Add onion and garlic; cook and stir

2 minutes. Add bell peppers and jalapeño
pepper; cook and stir 2 minutes. Stir in cumin;
cook and stir 1 minute.

4. Stir in chicken broth, rice and ham. Bring to
a boil over high heat. Reduce heat to low;
simmer, covered, 35 minutes.

5. Add peas; simmer 10 minutes or until liquid
is absorbed. Stir tomatoes and cilantro into
rice mixture just before serving.

Makes 6 servings

Country Recipe Biscuits

2 **cups all-purpose flour**
1 **tablespoon baking powder**
½ **cup prepared HIDDEN VALLEY® Original
    Ranch® salad dressing**
½ **cup buttermilk**

Preheat oven to 425°F. In small bowl, sift
together flour and baking powder. Make a well
in flour mixture; add salad dressing and
buttermilk. Stir with fork until dough forms a
ball. Drop by rounded spoonfuls onto
ungreased baking sheet. Bake until lightly
browned, 12 to 15 minutes.

Makes 12 biscuits

Southwest Hopping John

Honey Wheat Brown-and-Serve Rolls

    2 packages active dry yeast
    1 teaspoon sugar
    ¾ cup warm water (105° to 115°F)
    2 cups whole wheat flour
    2 to 3 cups all-purpose flour, divided
    ¼ cup vegetable shortening
    ¼ cup honey
    1 egg
    1 teaspoon salt

Sprinkle yeast and sugar over warm water in small bowl; stir until yeast is dissolved. Let stand 5 minutes or until mixture is bubbly. Combine whole wheat flour and 2 cups all-purpose flour in medium bowl. Measure 1½ cups flour mixture into large bowl. Add yeast mixture, shortening, honey, egg and salt. Beat with electric mixer at low speed until smooth. Increase mixer speed to medium; beat 2 minutes. Reduce speed to low; beat in 1 cup flour mixture. Increase mixer speed to medium; beat 2 minutes. Stir in remaining flour mixture and enough additional all-purpose flour (about ¼ cup) to make a soft dough.

Turn dough out onto lightly floured surface. Knead 8 to 10 minutes or until smooth and elastic, adding more flour to prevent sticking, if necessary. Shape dough into ball; place in large greased bowl. Turn once to grease surface. Cover with clean kitchen towel. Let rise in warm place (80° to 85°F) about 1½ hours or until doubled in bulk. Punch down dough. Turn dough onto lightly floured surface. Knead dough briefly; cover. Let rest 15 minutes. Meanwhile, grease 24 muffin cups.

Divide dough into 24 pieces. Cut 1 piece into thirds. Roll each third into a ball. Place 3 balls in each muffin cup. Repeat with remaining dough. Cover and let rise in warm place about 30 minutes or until doubled in bulk.

Preheat oven to 275°F.* Bake 20 to 25 minutes or until rolls are set but not brown. Immediately remove rolls from muffin cups and cool completely on wire racks. Store in resealable plastic food storage bags in refrigerator or freezer.

To bake rolls, thaw if frozen. Preheat oven to 400°F. Grease large jelly-roll pan. Place rolls on jelly-roll pan. Bake 8 to 10 minutes or until golden brown.   *Makes 24 rolls*

*To bake rolls immediately, preheat oven to 375°F. Bake 15 to 20 minutes or until golden brown. Immediately remove from pan. Serve warm.

Honey Wheat Brown-and-Serve Rolls

Cranberry-Orange Relish

4 large oranges, divided
7 (½-pint) jelly jars with lids and screw bands
2 cups sugar
½ cup water
2 packages (12 ounces each) fresh cranberries, washed and drained

1. Remove peel from white part of 2 oranges in long strips with sharp paring knife, making sure there is no white pith on the peel. Stack strips; cut into thin slivers. Measure ¼ cup; set aside.

2. Add orange peel to 1 inch boiling water in 1-quart saucepan. Boil over medium heat 5 minutes. Drain; set aside. Peel remaining 2 oranges; discard peel. Remove white pith from all 4 oranges; discard pith. Separate oranges into sections. With fingers, remove pulp from membrane of each section over 2-cup measure to save juice, discarding membrane. Dice orange sections into same cup. Add additional water to orange mixture to make 2 cups, if necessary; set aside.

3. Wash jars, lids and bands. Leave jars in hot water. Place lids and bands in large pan of water.

4. Combine sugar and water in heavy 6-quart saucepan or Dutch oven. Bring to a boil over medium heat. Add reserved orange peel, orange mixture and cranberries. Bring to a boil, stirring occasionally. Boil about 10 minutes or until mixture thickens and cranberries pop.

5. Bring water with lids and bands to a boil. Ladle hot mixture into hot jars, leaving ½-inch space at top. Run metal spatula around inside of jar to remove air bubbles. Wipe tops and sides of jar rims clean. Place hot lids and bands on jars. Screw bands tightly, but do not force. To process, place jars in boiling water; boil 10 minutes. Remove jars with tongs; cool on wire racks. (Check seals by pressing on lid with fingertip; lid should remain concave.) Label and date jars. Store unopened jars in a cool, dry place up to 12 months. Refrigerate up to 6 months after opening.

Makes about 7 (½-pint) jars

Golden Corn Pudding

2 tablespoons butter or margarine
3 tablespoons all-purpose flour
1 can (14¾ ounces) DEL MONTE® Cream Style Golden Sweet Corn
¼ cup yellow cornmeal
2 eggs, separated
1 package (3 ounces) cream cheese, softened
1 can (8¾ ounces) DEL MONTE® Whole Kernel Golden Sweet Corn, drained

1. Preheat oven to 350°F.

2. Melt butter in medium saucepan. Add flour and stir until smooth. Blend in cream style corn and cornmeal. Bring to a boil over medium heat, stirring constantly.

3. Place egg yolks in small bowl; stir in ½ cup hot mixture. Pour mixture back into saucepan. Add cream cheese and whole kernel corn.

4. Place egg whites in clean narrow bowl and beat until stiff peaks form. With rubber spatula, gently fold egg whites into corn mixture.

5. Pour mixture into 1½-quart straight-sided baking dish. Bake 30 to 35 minutes or until lightly browned.   *Makes 4 to 6 servings*

Tip: Pudding can be prepared up to 3 hours ahead of serving time. Cover and refrigerate until about 30 minutes before baking.

Prep Time: 10 minutes
Bake Time: 35 minutes

Ranch Mashed Potatoes

4 medium all-purpose potatoes, peeled, if desired, and cut into chunks (about 2 pounds)
1 envelope LIPTON® RECIPE SECRETS® Ranch Soup Mix
½ cup sour cream
½ cup milk
2 tablespoons margarine or butter, softened
2 slices bacon, crisp-cooked and crumbled or 2 tablespoons bacon bits (optional)

1. In 3-quart saucepan, cover potatoes with water. Bring to a boil.

2. Reduce heat to low and simmer 20 minutes or until potatoes are very tender; drain.

3. Return potatoes to saucepan; mash. Stir in remaining ingredients.   *Makes 6 servings*

Prep Time: 10 minutes
Cook Time: 25 minutes

Harvest Stuffing Bread

   3 cups all-purpose flour
   1 tablespoon sugar
   1 envelope FLEISCHMANN'S® RapidRise™
     Yeast
   2 tablespoons plus 1 teaspoon instant
     minced onions
   1 tablespoon parsley flakes
1½ teaspoons poultry seasoning
   1 teaspoon salt
1¼ cups water
   1 tablespoon butter or margarine
   1 egg, beaten
  ½ teaspoon whole celery seed

In large bowl, combine 2 cups flour, sugar, undissolved yeast, 2 tablespoons onions, parsley flakes, poultry seasoning and salt. Heat water and butter until very warm (120° to 130°F). Stir into dry ingredients. Beat 2 minutes at medium speed of electric mixer, scraping bowl occasionally. Stir in remaining flour to make stiff batter. Cover; let rest 10 minutes.

Turn batter into greased 1½-quart casserole. Smooth top of dough in casserole with floured hands. Cover; let rise in warm, draft-free place until doubled in size, about 30 minutes. Brush beaten egg on loaf. Sprinkle with remaining

onions and celery seed. Bake at 375°F* for 35 minutes or until done. Remove from casserole; cool on wire rack.

Makes 1 loaf

*Bake at 350°F if glass casserole is used.

Sweet Glazed Carrots

   1 pound fresh whole baby carrots, peeled
 ⅓ cup orange marmalade
 ¼ cup water
   1 tablespoon butter or margarine
   1 teaspoon LAWRY'S® Seasoned Salt

In medium saucepan, place ½ cup water. With steamer insert, steam carrots over boiling water until crisp-tender; drain. Remove steamer insert. Remove carrots to serving bowl. Immediately stir in remaining ingredients.   *Makes 4 to 5 servings*

Serving Suggestion: Serve with broiled or grilled fish, poultry or beef.

Hint: Substitute 1 package (16 ounces) frozen crinkle-cut carrots or 1 pound fresh carrots, thinly sliced, for baby carrots.

Harvest Stuffing Bread

Oven-Roasted Peppers and Onions

   Olive oil cooking spray
2 medium green bell peppers
2 medium red bell peppers
2 medium yellow bell peppers
4 small onions
1 teaspoon Italian herb seasoning
½ teaspoon dried basil leaves
¼ teaspoon ground cumin

1. Preheat oven to 375°F. Spray 15×10-inch jelly-roll pan with cooking spray. Cut bell peppers into 1½-inch pieces. Cut onions into quarters. Place vegetables on prepared pan. Spray vegetables with cooking spray. Bake 20 minutes; stir. Sprinkle with herb blend, basil and cumin.

2. *Increase oven temperature to 425°F.* Bake 20 minutes or until edges are darkened and vegetables are crisp-tender.

Makes 6 servings

Holiday Fruit and Nut Mold

  2 cups boiling water
1 package (8-serving size) or 2 packages (4-serving size) JELL-O® Brand Gelatin Dessert, any flavor
1¼ cups cold ginger ale or lemon-lime carbonated beverage
⅛ teaspoon ground cinnamon
⅛ teaspoon ground cloves
⅛ teaspoon ground nutmeg
½ cup chopped mixed dried fruit
⅓ cup currants or golden raisins
⅓ cup chopped candied or maraschino cherries
⅓ cup toasted chopped pecans or walnuts

STIR boiling water into gelatin in large bowl at least 2 minutes until completely dissolved. Stir in cold ginger ale and spices. Refrigerate about 1½ hours or until thickened (spoon drawn through leaves definite impression).

STIR in fruits and nuts. Spoon into 5-cup mold.

REFRIGERATE 4 hours or until firm. Unmold.

Makes 10 servings

Preparation Time: 20 minutes
Refrigerating Time: 5½ hours

Orange and Green Salad

**3 slices whole wheat bread, cut into
    ½-inch cubes
  Olive oil cooking spray
1 clove garlic, minced
3 tablespoons frozen orange juice
    concentrate, thawed
3 tablespoons balsamic vinegar
2 teaspoons honey
1 clove garlic, crushed
½ teaspoon grated orange peel
½ teaspoon olive oil
6 cups torn washed mixed salad greens,
    such as escarole, chicory, arugula,
    radicchio, romaine, spinach and
    watercress
2 navel oranges, peeled, seeded and cut
    into thin slices
½ cup thinly sliced red onion**

Preheat oven to 250°F. For croutons, spread
bread cubes in shallow baking pan. Coat
lightly with cooking spray; sprinkle with
minced garlic. Bake 10 minutes. Stir bread
cubes; coat lightly with cooking spray. Bake
5 minutes more or until croutons are browned
and crisp. Let cool to room temperature.

For dressing, combine orange juice
concentrate, vinegar, honey, crushed garlic,
orange peel and oil in medium bowl until
smooth. Let stand, covered, 1 hour to allow
flavors to blend.

Combine salad greens, oranges and onion in
large bowl. Just before serving, remove garlic
clove from dressing. Pour dressing over salad;
toss gently to coat. Sprinkle with croutons.

Makes 6 servings

Note: Dressing may be stored, covered, in
refrigerator up to 4 days.

Down-Home  Desserts

Holiday Fruit Cake

- **1 pound diced candied mixed fruits**
- **8 ounces candied cherries, cut into halves**
- **4 ounces candied pineapple, chopped**
- **1½ cups chopped nuts**
- **1 cup raisins**
- **½ cup all-purpose flour**
- **1 package DUNCAN HINES® Moist Deluxe® Spice Cake Mix**
- **1 (4-serving size) package vanilla-flavor instant pudding and pie filling mix**
- **3 eggs**
- **½ cup vegetable oil**
- **¼ cup water**
  Light corn syrup, heated, for garnish

Preheat oven to 300°F. Grease 10-inch tube pan. Line bottom with aluminum foil.

Reserve ¼ cup assorted candied fruits and nuts for garnish, if desired. Combine remaining candied fruits, nuts and raisins in large bowl. Toss with flour until evenly coated. Set aside.

Combine cake mix, pudding mix, eggs, oil and water in large mixing bowl. Beat at medium speed with electric mixer for 3 minutes (batter will be very stiff). Stir in candied fruit mixture. Spread in prepared pan. Bake 2 hours or until toothpick inserted in center comes out clean. Cool completely in pan. Invert onto serving plate. Peel off foil.

Brush cake with hot corn syrup and decorate with reserved candied fruit pieces and nuts, if desired. To store, wrap in aluminum foil or plastic wrap, or place in airtight container.

Makes 20 to 24 servings

Holiday Fruit Cake

Classic Rhubarb Pie

Crust
> Classic CRISCO® Double Crust (recipe follows)

Filling
> 4 cups red rhubarb, cut into ½- to ¾-inch pieces
> 1⅓ to 1½ cups sugar, to taste
> ⅓ cup all-purpose flour
> 2 tablespoons butter or margarine

Glaze
> 1 tablespoon milk
> Sugar

1. For crust, prepare crust as directed and press bottom crust into 9-inch pie plate, leaving overhang. Do not bake. Heat oven to 400°F.

2. For filling, combine rhubarb and sugar in large bowl. Mix well. Stir in flour. Spoon into unbaked pie crust. Dot with butter. Moisten pastry edge with water.

3. Cover pie with woven lattice top. Trim ½ inch beyond edge of pie plate. Fold top edge under bottom crust. Flute.

4. For glaze, brush with milk. Sprinkle with sugar. Cover edge with foil to prevent overbrowning. Bake at 400°F for 20 minutes.

Reduce oven temperature to 325°F. Remove foil. Bake 30 minutes or until filling in center is bubbly and crust is golden brown (if using frozen rhubarb, bake 60 to 70 minutes). *Do not overbake.* Cool until barely warm or to room temperature before serving.

Makes 1 (9-inch) pie

Classic Crisco® Double Crust

> 2 cups all-purpose flour
> 1 teaspoon salt
> ¾ Crisco® Stick or ¾ cup Crisco® all-vegetable shortening
> 5 tablespoons cold water (or more as needed)

1. Spoon flour into measuring cup and level. Combine flour and salt in medium bowl.

2. Cut in ¾ cup shortening using pastry blender or 2 knives until all flour is blended to form pea-size chunks.

continued on page 54

Classic Rhubarb Pie

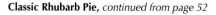

Classic Rhubarb Pie, *continued from page 52*

3. Sprinkle with water, 1 tablespoon at a time. Toss lightly with fork until dough forms a ball. Divide dough in half.

4. Press dough between hands to form 5- to 6-inch "pancake." Flour rolling surface and rolling pin lightly. Roll both halves of dough into circle. Trim one circle of dough 1 inch larger than upside-down pie plate. Carefully remove trimmed dough. Set aside to reroll and use for pastry cutout garnish, if desired.

5. Fold dough into quarters. Unfold and press into pie plate.

Christmas Rainbow Cake

    1 package (2-layer size) white cake mix
    1 package (4-serving size) JELL-O® Brand Lime Flavor Gelatin
    1 package (4-serving size) JELL-O® Brand Strawberry Flavor Gelatin
    2 tubs (8 ounces each) COOL WHIP® Whipped Topping, thawed

HEAT oven to 350°F.

PREPARE cake mix as directed on package. Divide batter equally between 2 bowls. Add lime gelatin to one bowl and strawberry gelatin to the other bowl. Stir until well blended. Pour each color batter into separate greased and floured 9-inch round cake pans.

BAKE 25 to 30 minutes or until toothpick inserted in center comes out clean. Cool 10 minutes; remove from pans. Cool to room temperature on wire racks.

SLICE each cooled cake layer in half horizontally. Place 1 lime-flavored cake layer on serving plate; frost with whipped topping. Top with 1 strawberry-flavored cake layer; frost with whipped topping. Repeat layers. Frost top and side of cake with remaining whipped topping. *Makes 10 to 12 servings*

Christmas Rainbow Cake

Fudgy Milk Chocolate Fondue

1 (16-ounce) can chocolate-flavored syrup
1 (14-ounce) can EAGLE® BRAND
    Sweetened Condensed Milk (NOT
    evaporated milk)
    Dash salt
1½ teaspoons vanilla extract
    Dippers: fresh fruit, cookies, pound cake
    cubes, angel food cake cubes

1. In heavy saucepan over medium heat, combine syrup, Eagle Brand and salt. Cook and stir 12 to 15 minutes or until slightly thickened.

2. Remove from heat; stir in vanilla. Serve warm with Dippers. Store covered in refrigerator.   *Makes about 3 cups*

Microwave Directions: In 1-quart glass measure, combine syrup, Eagle Brand and salt. Cook on 100% power (HIGH) 3½ to 4 minutes, stirring after 2 minutes. Stir in vanilla.

Tip: Can be served warm or cold over ice cream. Can be made several weeks ahead. Store tightly covered in refrigerator.

Prep Time: 12 to 15 minutes

Festive Mincemeat Tartlets

    Pastry for double pie crust
1½ cups prepared mincemeat
    ½ cup chopped peeled, cored tart apple
    ⅓ cup golden raisins
    ⅓ cup chopped walnuts
    3 tablespoons brandy or frozen apple juice
        concentrate, thawed
    1 tablespoon grated lemon peel

Preheat oven to 400°F. Divide pastry in half. Refrigerate one half. Roll remaining half on lightly floured surface to form 13-inch circle. Cut six 4-inch rounds. Fit each round into 2¾-inch muffin cup. Prick inside of crust with fork; set aside. Repeat with remaining pastry.

Bake unfilled pastry crusts 8 minutes. Meanwhile, combine mincemeat, apple, raisins, walnuts, brandy and lemon peel in medium bowl until well blended. Remove crusts from oven; fill each with rounded tablespoonful of mincemeat mixture. Press lightly into crust with back of spoon.

Bake 18 to 20 minutes more or until crust edges are golden. Cool in pan 5 minutes. Carefully remove from pan to wire rack. Serve warm or cool completely.

Makes 12 tartlets

Fudgy Milk Chocolate Fondue

Perfect Pumpkin Pie

1 (15-ounce) can pumpkin (2 cups)
1 (14-ounce) can EAGLE® BRAND Sweetened Condensed Milk (NOT evaporated milk)
2 eggs
1 teaspoon ground cinnamon
½ teaspoon ground ginger
½ teaspoon ground nutmeg
½ teaspoon salt
1 (9-inch) unbaked pie crust
Favorite Topping (recipes follow, optional)

1. Preheat oven to 425°F. In large bowl, combine all ingredients except pie crust; mix well.

2. Pour into prepared pie crust. Bake 15 minutes.

3. Reduce oven heat to 350°F. Continue baking 35 to 40 minutes, or as directed with one Favorite Topping, or until knife inserted 1 inch from edge comes out clean. Cool. Garnish as desired. Store covered in refrigerator. *Makes 1 (9-inch) pie*

Sour Cream Topping: In medium bowl, combine 1½ cups sour cream, 2 tablespoons sugar and 1 teaspoon vanilla extract. After pie has baked 30 minutes at 350°F, spread evenly over top; bake 10 minutes.

Streusel Topping: In medium bowl, combine ½ cup packed brown sugar and ½ cup all-purpose flour; cut in ¼ cup (½ stick) cold butter or margarine until crumbly. Stir in ¼ cup chopped nuts. After pie has baked 30 minutes at 350°F, sprinkle evenly over top; bake 10 minutes.

Chocolate Glaze: In small saucepan over low heat, melt ½ cup semi-sweet chocolate chips and 1 teaspoon solid shortening. Drizzle or spread over top of baked and cooled pie.

Prep Time: 20 minutes
Bake Time: 50 to 55 minutes

Sweet Potato Meringue Pie

1 (9-inch) graham cracker crust

Filling
**2 whole sweet potatoes or 1 (29-ounce)
    can sweet potatoes, drained**
**1 cup (12-ounce jar) SMUCKER'S® Sweet
    Orange Marmalade**
2 egg yolks
¼ teaspoon cinnamon
¼ teaspoon ginger
⅛ teaspoon allspice
⅛ teaspoon nutmeg
    Pinch of salt
1 cup evaporated skim milk
3 tablespoons cornstarch

Meringue
3 egg whites
    Pinch of salt
⅓ cup sugar

Bake graham cracker crust at 400°F for
10 minutes.

Meanwhile, pierce sweet potatoes with fork;
microwave on HIGH for 4 minutes. Combine
cooked sweet potatoes, marmalade, egg yolks,
cinnamon, ginger, allspice, nutmeg and salt;
stir to blend thoroughly. Stir in evaporated
milk. Add cornstarch and stir until smooth.

Pour filling into pie crust. Bake at 400°F for
45 to 55 minutes or until knife inserted in
center comes out clean. Remove pie from
oven and set aside to cool. Reduce oven heat
to 350°F.

Beat egg whites and salt with electric mixer
until soft peaks form. Gradually add sugar;
beat until egg whites are stiff and shiny.
Carefully spread meringue over top of cooled
pie. Bake at 350°F for 15 minutes or until
meringue is golden brown.

Cool pie on wire rack. Serve at room
temperature or refrigerate and serve cold.

Makes 10 servings

Fluted Chocolate-Maraschino Cake

- ⅔ **cup butter or margarine, softened**
- 1¾ **cups sugar**
- 2 **eggs**
- 1¼ **teaspoons almond extract**
- 1 **teaspoon vanilla extract**
- 1¾ **cups all-purpose flour**
- ¾ **cup HERSHEY'S Dutch Processed Cocoa**
- 1½ **teaspoons baking soda**
- 1½ **cups dairy sour cream**
  - **Powdered sugar**
  - **Cherry Whipped Cream (recipe follows)**
  - **Maraschino cherries (optional)**

1. Heat oven to 350°F. Grease and flour 12-cup fluted tube pan.

2. Beat butter and sugar in large bowl until creamy. Add eggs, almond and vanilla extracts; beat well. Combine flour, cocoa and baking soda; add to butter mixture alternately with sour cream, beating well. Pour into pan.

3. Bake 45 to 50 minutes or until wooden pick inserted into center comes out clean. Cool 15 minutes; remove from pan to wire rack. Cool completely. Sift with powdered sugar. Garnish with Cherry Whipped Cream and maraschino cherries, if desired. *Makes 12 servings*

Cherry Whipped Cream: Beat 1 cup whipping cream, 3 tablespoons powdered sugar, ½ teaspoon almond extract and ¼ teaspoon vanilla extract in medium bowl until stiff. Stir in ½ cup chopped maraschino cherries. Makes about 1 cup.

Fluted Chocolate-Maraschino Cake

Santa's Sweet Treats

Creamy Caramels

- ½ cup slivered or chopped toasted almonds (optional)
- 1 cup butter or margarine, cut into small pieces
- 1 can (14 ounces) sweetened condensed milk
- 2 cups sugar
- 1 cup light corn syrup
- 1½ teaspoons vanilla

Line 8-inch square baking pan with foil, extending edges over sides of pan. Lightly grease foil; sprinkle almonds over bottom of pan, if desired.

Melt butter in heavy 2-quart saucepan over low heat. Add milk, sugar and corn syrup. Stir over low heat until sugar is dissolved and mixture comes to a boil. Carefully clip candy thermometer to side of pan (do not let bulb touch bottom of pan). Cook over low heat about 30 minutes or until thermometer registers 240°F (soft-ball stage), stirring occasionally. Immediately remove from heat and stir in vanilla. Pour mixture into prepared pan. Cool completely.

Lift caramels out of pan using foil; remove foil. Place on cutting board; cut into 1-inch squares with sharp knife. Wrap each square in plastic wrap. Store in airtight container.

Makes about 2½ pounds or 64 caramels

Marbled Caramels: Before cooling, add ⅓ cup chocolate chips to top. Let soften; swirl lightly into caramel using a knife.

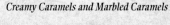

Creamy Caramels and Marbled Caramels

Double Chocolate Cookies

- 2 cups biscuit baking mix
- 1 (14-ounce) can EAGLE® BRAND Sweetened Condensed Milk (NOT evaporated milk)
- 8 (1-ounce) squares semi-sweet chocolate or 1 (12-ounce) package semi-sweet chocolate chips, melted
- 3 tablespoons butter or margarine, melted
- 1 egg
- 1 teaspoon vanilla extract
- 6 (1¼-ounce) white chocolate candy bars with almonds, broken into small pieces
- ¾ cup chopped nuts

1. Preheat oven to 350°F. In large bowl, combine all ingredients except candy pieces and nuts; beat until smooth.

2. Stir in remaining ingredients. Drop by rounded teaspoonfuls, 2 inches apart, onto ungreased baking sheets.

3. Bake 10 minutes or until tops are slightly crusted (do not overbake). Cool. Store tightly covered at room temperature.

Makes about 4½ dozen

Mint Chocolate Cookies: Substitute ¾ cup mint-flavored chocolate chips for white chocolate candy bars with almonds. Proceed as directed above.

Chocolate Raspberry Truffles

- 1 (14-ounce) can EAGLE® BRAND Sweetened Condensed Milk (NOT evaporated milk)
- ¼ cup raspberry liqueur
- 2 tablespoons butter or margarine
- 2 tablespoons seedless raspberry jam
- 2 (12-ounce) packages semi-sweet chocolate chips
- ½ cup powdered sugar or ground toasted almonds

1. Microwave first 4 ingredients in large microwave-safe bowl on HIGH (100% power) 3 minutes.

2. Stir in chips until smooth. Cover and chill 1 hour.

3. Shape mixture into 1-inch balls and roll in powdered sugar or almonds. Store covered at room temperature.

Makes 4 dozen

Prep Time: 10 minutes
Cook Time: 3 minutes
Chill Time: 1 hour

Left to right: Chocolate Raspberry Truffles, Double Chocolate Cookies

Berlinerkranser (Little Wreaths)

1 cup Butter Flavor CRISCO® all-vegetable
shortening or 1 Butter Flavor CRISCO®
Stick
1 cup confectioners' sugar
2 large hard boiled egg yolks, mashed
2 large eggs, separated
1 teaspoon vanilla
1 teaspoon almond extract
2¼ cups all-purpose flour
Green colored sugar crystals
12 red candied cherries, cut into halves

1. Combine shortening and confectioners' sugar in large bowl. Beat on medium speed with electric mixer until well blended. Beat in hard boiled egg yolks, uncooked egg yolks, vanilla and almond extract. Beat in flour, ¼ cup at a time, until well blended. Cover and refrigerate 3 hours.

2. Let dough stand at room temperature until it becomes easy to handle.

3. Heat oven to 350°F. Divide dough into 2 equal portions. Cut each portion into 24 equal pieces. Roll each piece of dough into 5-inch-long rope. Form each rope into wreath or loop 1½ inches apart on ungreased cookie sheet, overlapping both ends. Brush each wreath with beaten egg whites; sprinkle with colored sugar crystals. Lightly press cherry piece into top of each wreath.

4. Bake at 350°F for 10 to 12 minutes or until edges are lightly browned. Cool on cookie sheets 3 minutes; transfer to cooling racks.

Makes about 4 dozen cookies

Berlinerkranser (Little Wreaths)

White Chocolate Cranberry Biscotti

2 cups flour
1½ teaspoons CALUMET® Baking Powder
¼ teaspoon salt
½ cup (1 stick) butter *or* margarine, softened
½ cup sugar
2 eggs
1 teaspoon vanilla
1 package (12 ounces) BAKER'S® White Chocolate Chunks, divided
½ cup dried cranberries
½ cup chopped pecans (optional)

HEAT oven to 325°F. Lightly grease and flour large cookie sheet. Mix flour, baking powder and salt in medium bowl; set aside.

BEAT butter and sugar in large bowl with electric mixer on medium speed until light and fluffy. Add eggs and vanilla; beat well. Gradually beat in flour mixture. Stir in 1½ cups of the chocolate chunks, cranberries and pecans.

DIVIDE dough into 2 equal portions. On floured board, shape dough into 2 logs, each 14 inches long, 1½ inches wide and 1 inch thick. Place 2 inches apart on prepared cookie sheet.

BAKE 25 to 28 minutes or until lightly browned. Cool on cookie sheet 15 minutes. On cutting board, cut each log with serrated knife into diagonal slices about ¾ inch thick. Place slices, cut sides down, on cookie sheet ½ inch apart. Bake 10 minutes or until slightly dry. Remove to wire racks and cool completely.

MELT remaining chocolate chunks as directed on package. Drizzle over biscotti. Let stand until chocolate is firm.

Makes about 3 dozen

Storage Know-How: Store in tightly covered container up to 2 weeks.

Prep Time: 30 minutes
Bake Time: 38 minutes

Fast and Easy Microwave Peanut Brittle

- 1 cup granulated sugar
- ½ cup light corn syrup
- 2 tablespoons water
- ⅛ teaspoon salt
- 1¼ cups Spanish peanuts
- 1 tablespoon butter or margarine
- 1 teaspoon baking soda

Microwave Directions

In 2½ quart microwavable mixing bowl, combine sugar, corn syrup, water and salt; stir well. Cook uncovered on HIGH 5 minutes. Stir in peanuts and cook uncovered 3 to 5 minutes or until syrup reaches hard crack stage and is lightly golden in color. (The hard crack stage is achieved when a little candy syrup dropped into ice water separates into hard, brittle threads.) Remove from microwave; stir in butter and baking soda. Pour mixture onto oiled baking sheet, spreading to ¼-inch thickness. When cool, break into pieces and store in airtight container.   *Makes 1 pound*

Favorite recipe from **The Sugar Association, Inc.**

Spicy Pumpkin Cookies

- 2 CRISCO® Sticks or 2 cups CRISCO® all-vegetable shortening
- 2 cups sugar
- 1 can (16 ounces) solid pack pumpkin
- 2 eggs
- 2 teaspoons vanilla
- 4 cups all-purpose flour
- 2 teaspoons baking powder
- 2 teaspoons ground cinnamon
- 1 teaspoon salt
- 1 teaspoon baking soda
- 1 teaspoon ground nutmeg
- ½ teaspoon ground allspice
- 2 cups raisins
- 1 cup chopped nuts

1. Heat oven to 350°F. Combine shortening, sugar, pumpkin, eggs and vanilla in large bowl; beat well.

2. Combine flour, baking powder, cinnamon, salt, baking soda, nutmeg and allspice in medium bowl. Add to pumpkin mixture; mix well. Stir in raisins and nuts. Drop rounded teaspoonfuls of dough, 2 inches apart, onto greased cookie sheet.

3. Bake at 350°F for 12 to 15 minutes. Cool on wire rack. If desired, frost with vanilla frosting.   *Makes about 7 dozen cookies*

English Thumbprint Cookies

   1 cup pecan pieces
1¼ cups all-purpose flour
  ¼ teaspoon salt
  ½ cup butter, softened
  ½ cup firmly packed light brown sugar
   1 teaspoon vanilla
   1 large egg, separated
   2 to 3 tablespoons seedless raspberry or
      strawberry jam

1. Preheat oven to 350°F. To toast pecans, spread on ungreased baking sheet. Bake 8 to 10 minutes or until golden brown, stirring frequently. Remove pecans from baking sheet and cool. Process cooled pecans in food processor until finely chopped; transfer to shallow bowl.

2. Place flour and salt in medium bowl; stir to combine. Beat butter and brown sugar in large bowl with electric mixer at medium speed until light and fluffy. Beat in vanilla and egg yolk. Gradually beat in flour mixture. Beat egg white with fork until frothy.

3. Shape dough into 1-inch balls. Roll balls in egg white; roll in nuts to coat. Place balls on ungreased cookie sheets. Press deep indentation in center of each ball with thumb.

4. Bake 8 minutes or until set. Remove cookies from oven; fill each indentation with about ¼ teaspoon jam. Return filled cookies to oven; continue to bake 8 to 10 minutes or until lightly brown. Immediately remove cookies to wire racks; cool completely.

5. Store cookies tightly covered at room temperature or freeze up to 3 months.
Makes about 2½ dozen cookies

English Thumbprint Cookies

Luscious Fresh Lemon Bars

Crust
- ½ **cup butter or margarine, softened**
- ½ **cup granulated sugar**
  - **Grated peel of ½ SUNKIST® lemon**
- 1¼ **cups all-purpose flour**

Lemon Layer
- 4 **eggs**
- 1⅔ **cups granulated sugar**
- 3 **tablespoons all-purpose flour**
- ½ **teaspoon baking powder**
  - **Grated peel of ½ SUNKIST® lemon**
  - **Juice of 2 SUNKIST® lemons**
    - **(6 tablespoons)**
- 1 **teaspoon vanilla extract**
  - **Confectioners' sugar**

To make crust, in bowl blend together butter, granulated sugar and lemon peel. Gradually stir in flour to form a soft crumbly dough. Press evenly into bottom of foil-lined 13×9×2-inch baking pan. Bake at 350°F for 15 minutes.

Meanwhile, to prepare lemon layer, in large bowl whisk or beat eggs well. Stir together granulated sugar, flour and baking powder. Gradually whisk sugar mixture into beaten eggs. Stir or whisk in lemon peel, lemon juice and vanilla. Pour over hot baked crust. Return to oven and bake for 20 to 25 minutes, or until top and sides are lightly browned. Cool. Using foil on two sides, lift out the cookie base and gently loosen foil along all sides. With a long wet knife, cut into bars or squares. Sprinkle tops with confectioners' sugar.

Makes about 3 dozen bars

Dark Chocolate Fudge

- ½ cup light *or* dark corn syrup
- ⅓ cup evaporated milk *or* whipping (heavy) cream
- 2 packages (8 squares each) BAKER'S® Semi-Sweet Baking Chocolate
- ¾ cup powdered sugar, sifted
- 2 teaspoons vanilla
- 1 cup coarsely chopped nuts (optional)

LINE 8-inch square baking pan with foil; grease foil.

HEAT corn syrup, evaporated milk and chocolate in 2-quart saucepan on medium-low heat until chocolate is melted, stirring constantly. Remove from heat.

STIR in sugar, vanilla and nuts. Beat with wooden spoon until thick and glossy. Immediately spread in prepared pan.

REFRIGERATE 2 hours or until firm. Let stand at room temperature 15 minutes before cutting into 1-inch squares.   *Makes 64 pieces*

Make-Ahead: Can be prepared up to 3 weeks ahead for gift-giving. Store in an airtight container between layers of wax paper in the refrigerator.

Almond Lace Cookies

- ¼ cup butter, softened
- ½ cup sugar
- ½ cup BLUE DIAMOND® Blanched Almond Paste
- ¼ cup all-purpose flour
- 2 tablespoons milk
- 2 teaspoons grated orange peel
- ½ teaspoon almond extract
- ¼ teaspoon salt

Cream butter and sugar. Beat in almond paste. Add remaining ingredients. Mix well. Drop rounded teaspoonfuls onto cookie sheet, 3 inches apart. (Cookies will spread.) Bake at 350°F for 8 to 10 minutes or until edges are lightly browned. Cool 3 to 4 minutes on cookie sheet; remove and cool on wire rack.

Makes 1½ dozen cookies

Acknowledgments

The publisher would like to thank the companies and organizations listed below for the use of their recipes and photographs in this publication.

American Lamb Council
Blue Diamond Growers®
Cherry Marketing Institute
ConAgra Grocery Products Company
Del Monte Corporation
Dole Food Company, Inc.
Duncan Hines® and Moist Deluxe® are
registered trademarks of Aurora Foods Inc.
Eagle® Brand
Egg Beaters®
Fleischmann's® Yeast
Hershey Foods Corporation
Holland House® is a registered trademark of Mott's, Inc.
The HV Company
Kraft Foods Holdings
Lawry's® Foods, Inc.
McIlhenny Company (TABASCO® brand Pepper Sauce)
Mott's® is a registered trademark of Mott's, Inc.
Mushroom Council
Norseland, Inc./Lucini Italia Co.
The Procter & Gamble Company
The J.M. Smucker Company
The Sugar Association, Inc.
Sunkist Growers
Tyson Foods, Inc.
Unilever Bestfoods North America

Index

METRIC CONVERSION CHART

VOLUME MEASUREMENTS (dry)

1/8 teaspoon = 0.5 mL
1/4 teaspoon = 1 mL
1/2 teaspoon = 2 mL
3/4 teaspoon = 4 mL
1 teaspoon = 5 mL
1 tablespoon = 15 mL
2 tablespoons = 30 mL
1/4 cup = 60 mL
1/3 cup = 75 mL
1/2 cup = 125 mL
2/3 cup = 150 mL
3/4 cup = 175 mL
1 cup = 250 mL
2 cups = 1 pint = 500 mL
3 cups = 750 mL
4 cups = 1 quart = 1 L

VOLUME MEASUREMENTS (fluid)

1 fluid ounce (2 tablespoons) = 30 mL
4 fluid ounces (1/2 cup) = 125 mL
8 fluid ounces (1 cup) = 250 mL
12 fluid ounces (1 1/2 cups) = 375 mL
16 fluid ounces (2 cups) = 500 mL

WEIGHTS (mass)

1/2 ounce = 15 g
1 ounce = 30 g
3 ounces = 90 g
4 ounces = 120 g
8 ounces = 225 g
10 ounces = 285 g
12 ounces = 360 g
16 ounces = 1 pound = 450 g

DIMENSIONS

1/16 inch = 2 mm
1/8 inch = 3 mm
1/4 inch = 6 mm
1/2 inch = 1.5 cm
3/4 inch = 2 cm
1 inch = 2.5 cm

OVEN TEMPERATURES

250°F = 120°C
275°F = 140°C
300°F = 150°C
325°F = 160°C
350°F = 180°C
375°F = 190°C
400°F = 200°C
425°F = 220°C
450°F = 230°C

BAKING PAN SIZES

Utensil	Size in Inches/Quarts	Metric Volume	Size in Centimeters
Baking or	8×8×2	2 L	20×20×5
Cake Pan	9×9×2	2.5 L	23×23×5
(square or	12×8×2	3 L	30×20×5
rectangular)	13×9×2	3.5 L	33×23×5
Loaf Pan	8×4×3	1.5 L	20×10×7
	9×5×3	2 L	23×13×7
Round Layer	8×1½	1.2 L	20×4
Cake Pan	9×1½	1.5 L	23×4
Pie Plate	8×1¼	750 mL	20×3
	9×1¼	1 L	23×3
Baking Dish	1 quart	1 L	—
or Casserole	1½ quart	1.5 L	—
	2 quart	2 L	—